EXCEPTIONAL ENGINEE

T0045336

EXTRAORDINARY SKYSCRAPERS

by Sonya Newland

CAPSTONE PRESS
a capstone imprint

Fact Finders Books are published by Capstone Press,
1710 Roe Crest Drive, North Mankato, Minnesota 56003
www.mycapstone.com

Produced for Capstone Publishers by
White-Thomson Publishing Ltd
www.wtpub.co.uk

Library of Congress Cataloging-in-Publication Data
Library of Congress Cataloging-in-Publication data is available on the Library of Congress website.
Names: Newland, Sonya, author.
Title: Extraordinary Skyscrapers: The Science of How and Why They Were Built/by Sonya Newland.
Description: North Mankato, Minnesota: Capstone Press, [2019] | Series: Fact Finders. Exceptional Engineering | Includes bibliographical references and index. | Audience: Ages 8–10.
Identifiers: LCCN 2018010611 (print) | LCCN 2018013667 (ebook) | ISBN 9781543529067 (library binding) | ISBN 9781543529111 (paperback)| ISBN 9781543529159 (eBook PDF)
Subjects: LCSH: Skyscrapers—History—Juvenile literature. | Structural engineering—Juvenile literature.
Classification: LCC TH1615 (ebook) | LCC TH1615 .N49 2019 (print) | DDC 720/.483—dc23
LC record available at https://lccn.loc.gov/2018010611

Editorial Credits
Editor: Sonya Newland
Designer: Steve Mead
Media Researcher: Sonya Newland
Production Specialist: Laura Manthe

Photo Credits

Alamy: Archive PL, 7, Kim Karpeles, 9, Aerial Archives, 15, View Pictures, 21, Oscar Elias, 29; Getty Images: View Pictures, 19, 20, Bloomberg, 23b, 27t; iStock: sx70, 4, rambo182, 5b, 25, Mienny, 12, superjoseph, 14, fotoVoyager, 16, mustafacan, 17, zorazhuang, 22, gionnixxx, 24, JunotPhotography, 26, EnginKorkmaz, 28; Library of Congress: 6, 8r, 8l; Steve Mead: 23t, 27b; Shutterstock: Rus S, cover, ONiONA_studio, 5t, Lucas Photo, 10, rarrarorro, 11, Sundy Photography, 13, Patrick Wang, 18.

Design elements by Shutterstock

Printed and bound in the United States of America.
PA021

TABLE OF CONTENTS

CHAPTER 1

FLATIRON BUILDING, NEW YORK

Since the first skyscraper was built more than 100 years ago, people have looked for ways to construct increasingly tall buildings. But it's not easy to build a structure that is both tall and safe. The materials used have to be incredibly strong. Because winds can be very dangerous up high, the building must be evenly balanced. However, **engineers** and architects have overcome these problems. Today, skyscrapers can be seen all over the world.

The Flatiron Building is 285 feet (87 meters) tall. It is not considered a skyscraper by today's standards, but it was when it was built.

engineer—someone trained to design and build machines, vehicles, bridges, roads, or other structures

New York City is filled with tall buildings. The Flatiron was one of the first skyscrapers in New York. Thanks to its unusual shape and design, it is also one of the most famous buildings in the city. When it was completed in 1902, newspapers called it "a monstrosity" and "a stingy piece of pie." But New Yorkers loved it!

The streets of New York were designed mainly in a grid pattern, like a tic-tac-toe board. However, some streets were built on an angle, which left a few odd-shaped pieces of land. The triangular strip where Fifth Avenue, Broadway, and 23rd Street meet was one of these places.

The Fuller Company bought this piece of land for its new headquarters. They hired famous architect Daniel Burnham, who designed an unusual building with a steel frame.

The northern point of the Flatiron Building is only 6.5 feet (2 m) wide. The offices in the point are triangular in shape.

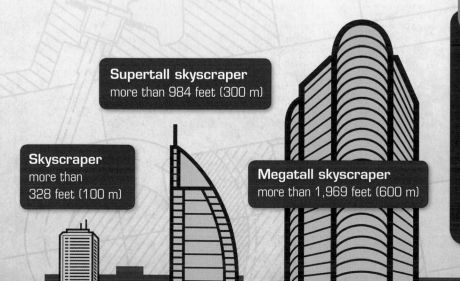

Supertall skyscraper
more than 984 feet (300 m)

Skyscraper
more than 328 feet (100 m)

Megatall skyscraper
more than 1,969 feet (600 m)

Did You Know?

The Empire State Building is another famous skyscraper in New York City. It opened in 1931 and was the tallest building in the world for nearly 40 years.

When people saw the Flatiron being built, they were afraid it would topple over. They thought the frame was too thin and the building was too narrow. But the steel frame was incredibly strong and could support a very tall building.

BALANCING WEIGHT IN A SKYSCRAPER

The weight of a skyscraper has to be spread out evenly throughout the building, otherwise the whole thing might collapse. To do this, engineers use three types of support—vertical columns, horizontal **girders**, and **diagonal** beams.

You can build a "skyscraper" using rectangular wooden blocks for the three types of support. Experiment by putting them in different places. What happens if one part is heavier than another? What pattern of columns and beams is the strongest?

Locals nicknamed the building the Flatiron because it was the same shape as an old-fashioned clothes iron.

girder—a large, heavy beam made of steel or concrete and used in construction
diagonal—joining opposite corners of a square or rectangle

The Flatiron Building went up quickly after the **foundation** was laid. After that, the floors were added at a rate of one per week. When it was finished, the building was 22 stories tall. No one wanted to climb all those stairs, so elevators were installed. The original elevators were **hydraulic**. They were replaced with computer-controlled elevators in the 21st century.

After the steel frame was in place, it took only four months to finish construction on the Flatiron Building.

foundation—a base on which something rests or is built
hydraulic—powered by fluid forced through pipes or chambers

CHAPTER 2

TRIBUNE TOWER, CHICAGO

Chicago is well-known for its groundbreaking skyscrapers. The Tribune Tower was one of the first—and one of the most famous—to be built in the city.

In 1922 the *Chicago Tribune* launched a design competition for its new headquarters. It asked for "the world's most beautiful office building" and offered a prize of $50,000 for the winning design. More than 260 ideas were sent in from all over the world, but one was the clear winner. It came from New York architects John Howells and Raymond Hood.

Did You Know?

Chicago was home to the world's first skyscraper. The Home Insurance Building was completed in 1885. It had 10 stories and was 138 feet (42 m) high. It was torn down in 1931.

Architects from all over the world entered the competition. These are two of the designs that did not win.

Work began on the tower in 1923. First the frame was constructed of steel and concrete, then the building was covered with **limestone**. Fragments of other famous buildings were sealed into the limestone. The Tribune Tower contains pieces of the Great Pyramid of Giza in Egypt, the Taj Mahal in India, and the Great Wall of China.

BUTTER TOWER
CATHEDRAL OF
NOTRE DAME
ROUEN, FRANCE

There are pieces of 150 other famous places embedded in the Tribune Tower.

THE WIND EFFECT

Skyscrapers have to be able to withstand high winds. Try to design a skyscraper that would stand strong in Chicago, "the Windy City." What basic shape would work best—square, rectangle, triangle, or circle? Use rolled-up newspaper and tape to build your skyscraper. Create different shapes by taping smaller newspaper rolls to a larger one. Then use a fan or a hairdryer to test the strength of your structure. Is it better to have a narrow top or a wide one? What about the base?

limestone—a hard rock formed from the remains of ancient sea creatures

Look at most buildings and you'll see they have squared-off corners. This gives them a sharp-edged, boxy look. Hood and Howells wanted something different for the Tribune Tower. They had the corners of the main block cut diagonally, which makes the building look smoother and narrower.

The Tribune Tower is 462 feet (141 m) high.

When the main tower was completed, it was 24 stories high—but there was more to come. An octagon-shaped tower on top of the lower block added another 10 stories. In all, there are 34 stories above ground and two below.

Hood and Howells' skyscraper was a mixture of old and new. The clean vertical lines of the lower tower were modern, but the architects also copied older styles. In particular they included many **Gothic** features, such as **flying buttresses**, spires, and **gargoyles**. The very top looks like a crown.

Gothic—a style of art or architecture used in western Europe between the 1100s and 1500s that featured tall towers, arches, and stained-glass windows

flying buttress—an arched structure that extends beyond a wall or building and supports it

gargoyle—an animal head or figure carved out of stone

Other decorative features on the Tribune Tower reflect a military theme. Beneath some of the windows are lead panels with images on them. These include symbols such as an eagle and a five-pointed star.

Did You Know?

The Tribune Tower also features carvings of Robin Hood and a howling dog. These honor the architects Hood and Howells.

The detailed carvings on the Tribune Tower were influenced by the style of a famous Gothic cathedral in Rouen, France.

CHAPTER 3

TRANSAMERICA PYRAMID, SAN FRANCISCO

In 1968 the Transamerica Company announced plans for a new headquarters in San Francisco, California. It would be 853 feet (260 m) tall and have 48 floors. The chosen design was for a building shaped like a tall, narrow pyramid. No one had seen anything like it before. People who lived in the city were horrified.

Locals may have objected at first, but they came to love the Transamerica Pyramid. This unusual skyscraper is still the tallest building in San Francisco.

The Transamerica Pyramid is covered in a crushed white stone called quartz. This gives it a pure white color.

All the windows in the Transamerica Pyramid are cleaned and polished several times a year.

Architect William Pereira did not choose a pyramid shape simply because he wanted his building to stand out. He chose this shape for environmental reasons too. Fog from San Francisco Bay often covers the city. Pereira wanted to make sure that the new skyscraper did not block out too much natural light. Because it is narrow at the top and wider at the bottom, a pyramid shape casts a smaller shadow than a rectangle. This allows more light to reach the streets below.

Did You Know?

The Transamerica Pyramid has 3,678 windows. Most of them can be rotated 360 degrees so that they can be washed from the inside.

Tall buildings need deep foundations. To provide a solid base for the Transamerica Pyramid, steel and concrete were sunk 52 feet (15.5 m) into the ground. Then a 9-foot (2.7-m) block of concrete was built on top. Around 1,750 truckloads of concrete were used. Concrete was poured nonstop for 24 hours.

The base of the Transamerica Pyramid is supported by a series of diagonal beams. These strengthen the building against earthquakes.

EARTHQUAKE SAFETY

San Francisco often experiences damaging earthquakes, so buildings have to be designed with safety in mind. The foundation of the Transamerica Pyramid moves when the earth shakes. There are also special rods in the structure that allow the building to move from side to side. During a major earthquake in 1989, the top of the Transamerica Pyramid swayed more than 12 inches (30.5 centimeters). However, the building was not damaged.

Near the top of the Transamerica Pyramid are two unusual features—a "wing" on each side. These were designed to solve a particular problem. Elevators could not run at the angle of the slope high up in the building. The wings contain elevator shafts so that people can travel to the top floors. Above the wings is an aluminum spire. This hollow cone is 212 feet (65 m) tall. The spire contains a steel staircase and ladders that go all the way to the top.

The spire is just for decoration—there are no offices at the top of the pyramid.

CHAPTER 4

PETRONAS TWIN TOWERS, KUALA LUMPUR

Until 1996 every building to hold the title of "world's tallest" had been in the United States. That changed when the Petronas Towers opened in Malaysia. The towers are 1,483 feet (452 m) high and contain 88 stories each.

The Petronas Towers are no longer the tallest buildings in the world, but they are still the tallest twin towers.

Buildings this tall need a very strong base. The foundations for the Petronas Towers are 98 feet (30 m) deep. It took 54 hours of continuous concrete pouring to create the foundation for each tower. After the foundations were laid, a basement level was built on top. A **retaining wall** was added to reinforce the whole lower area.

Two years later, work began on the **superstructure**. Architect Cesar Pelli chose a circular shape for the towers. Each one was surrounded by eight smaller columns. Usually buildings have a frame made of either steel or concrete, but Pelli used concrete that was **reinforced** with steel. When complete, the towers were covered in stainless steel and glass.

At the very top of each tower is a pyramid topped by a thin steel spire.

Did You Know?

The Twin Towers are joined at the 41st and 42nd floors by a double-decker "sky bridge." The bridge is attached to the towers by hinges. The hinges allow the bridge to slide in and out to avoid being damaged when the towers sway in the wind.

retaining wall—a wall that is built to keep the land behind it from sliding

superstructure—the part of a building that is above the foundation or lowest part

reinforce—to strengthen the structure or shape of something

CHAPTER 5

THE GHERKIN, LONDON

In 1992 a bomb went off in London, damaging several old buildings that had to be torn down. To replace the offices at 30 St Mary Axe, architect Sir Norman Foster designed a new skyscraper. The building was round, but it was narrower at the top and bottom than it was in the middle. The unusual shape soon earned it the nickname "the Gherkin" because it looks like a type of small pickle. Foster chose this shape because the building is located in London's busy and crowded financial district. The narrow base leaves more space on the ground.

Work began on the Gherkin in 2001. It opened in April 2004.

Did You Know?

When wind hits a building, some of it is forced downward. Wind flows more easily over a round surface than a flat one, so less is pushed down to the street below.

The Gherkin has a diagonal frame called a "diagrid." This is a network of steel tubes that crisscross each other to form a diamond pattern. Skyscrapers usually need columns inside them for support and to spread the weight. The strong outer frame of the Gherkin reduces the need for internal columns, leaving more space inside the building.

The Gherkin's strong steel frame protects the building from high winds.

3D MODELING

3D modeling—using 3D images on a computer—is a useful way to solve problems when designing buildings. Because of the curve of the building, every floor in the Gherkin is a slightly different size. For this reason, engineers used 3D modeling to figure out what size the diagrid needed to be at each level. 3D modeling allowed engineers to see how changes to the grid's size and position would affect the real building.

When the frame was completed, the building had 41 stories and stood 591 feet (180 m) tall. The next stage was to install the outer surface. Workers carefully covered the skyscraper in thick glass panels. All together 7,429 of these panels were placed in a diamond-shaped pattern. Although the building is round, it contains only one piece of curved glass. This piece is in the dome at the very top. The dome allows visitors a 360-degree view of London.

Did You Know?

There are 18 elevators in the Gherkin. They travel at speeds of 26 feet (8 m) per second and can carry a total of 378 people.

More than 258,000 square feet (24,000 square meters) of glass were used in building the Gherkin.

The Gherkin was the first skyscraper to be designed with environmental issues as a priority.

The Gherkin is very energy efficient. Open **shafts** were placed between each floor. These allow sunlight to spread throughout the building, which reduces electricity costs. The shafts also form a special **ventilation system**. This system removes warm air in the summer and draws heat from the sun into the building in the winter. This amazing skyscraper uses half the energy that most traditionally air-conditioned buildings do.

shaft—a long, narrow passage that goes straight down
ventilation system—a system that allows the flow of fresh air

CHAPTER 6

WORLD FINANCIAL CENTER, SHANGHAI

The World Financial Center in Shanghai, China, opened in 2008. At 1,614 feet (492 m), it was the second tallest skyscraper in the world at the time. Today it ranks 10th, beaten by the Shanghai Tower, among others. Together with the Jin Mao Tower, these three supertall buildings dominate the city skyline.

The World Financial Center (on the left) was the first of Shanghai's three supertall skyscrapers.

Did You Know?

The top of the World Financial Center is home to a five-star hotel. It has 174 rooms covering the 79th to 93rd floors of the building. The upper floors form the highest hotel in the world.

Work on the World Financial Center began in 1997. However, after the foundation was laid, the project was put on hold. With a financial crisis happening in Asia, there was no money to spend on skyscrapers.

By the time things picked up again in 2003, the plans had changed. The developers wanted an even taller building. Instead of 94 stories, they wanted 101. This would make it 105 feet (32 m) taller than originally planned. Reinforcing the foundation to deal with the extra height was going to be expensive. Instead, the engineers cleverly changed the design of the frame inside the building.

World Financial Center by the Numbers

HEIGHT:
1,614 feet (492 m)

OBSERVATION DECK HEIGHT:
1,555 feet (474 m)

PORTAL WIDTH:
164 feet (50 m)

AREA:
4,107,500 square feet
(381,600 square meters)

FLOORS:
104 (3 are below ground)

ELEVATORS:
91

PARKING SPACES:
1,100

COST:
$1.2 billion

The World Financial Center was built using a design that repeated itself every 13 floors. This repeated pattern made it quicker to construct. It also reduced the amount of wasted material used during the building process.

The most famous part of the World Financial Center is the hole at the top. But this "portal" is not just a nice design feature. It plays an important part in keeping the building stable. Instead of hitting the surface of the building, wind passes through the portal. This reduces the wind pressure at the top of this supertall structure.

Wind can also cause problems at ground level. It blows in from the entrance and up the building through elevator shafts and stairwells. This is called the "stack effect," and it can be noisy and damage the building. The World Financial Center has special outer lobbies that stop the wind from getting into the building.

The World Financial Center has been nicknamed "the bottle opener" because of the hole at the top.

Did You Know?

In the original plans, the space at the top of the building was a circle. But some people thought that it looked like the Japanese symbol of the rising sun. Instead, a trapezoid shape was chosen, which was easier to create than a circle.

BUILDING LOADS

When designing a building, engineers have to consider the forces, or loads, that will act on it. Forces include the weight of the building (called dead load) and all the objects and people inside it. They also include factors such as earthquakes, wind, and soil.

- Try out different loads on the skyscraper you built on page 6.

- Put items inside it to see how much weight it can bear.

- Build it on different materials, such as sand and rock, to see how this changes its strength.

- Build it on a tray, and then gently shake the tray to imitate an earthquake. Does it stand strong or collapse at the slightest tremor?

- Re-create winds using a fan or hairdryer at different speeds. How much wind can your building withstand?

- How could you change the design of your skyscraper to improve how much weight it can bear?

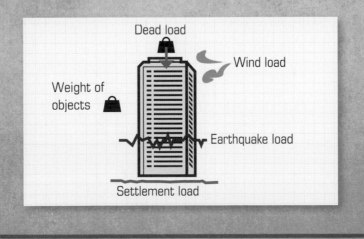

CHAPTER 7

BURJ KHALIFA, DUBAI

The Burj Khalifa is the tallest building in the world. At 2,723 feet (828 m), it was also the very first megatall skyscraper. Famous architects from all over the world sent in designs. The one that was chosen came from a firm called Skidmore, Owings & Merrill. They had designed the Sears Tower in Chicago—the world's tallest building from 1973 until 1998.

The foundation was set 164 feet (50 m) deep and used more than 120,000 tons (109,000 tonnes) of concrete. The concrete was reinforced with 192 **pilings** to add extra support for the huge structure.

The Burj Khalifa has 163 stories. It towers over the city of Dubai.

piling—a heavy wood or steel pole or beam that is driven into the ground to support a building, bridge, or pier

The body of the building was also made of reinforced concrete. However, this is not what you see when you look at it. The tower is covered with glass and panels made of aluminum and stainless steel. These make it shimmer in the desert sunshine. Because of the high temperatures, special glass had to be used to keep heat out of the building.

Work began on the Burj Khalifa in 2004. It opened in 2010.

The 10 Tallest Buildings in the World

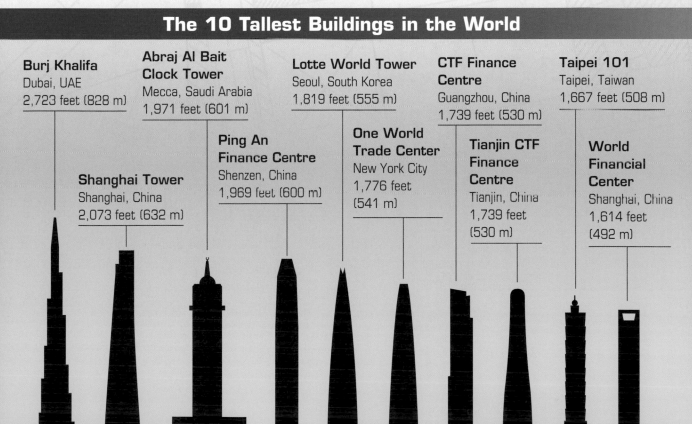

Burj Khalifa
Dubai, UAE
2,723 feet (828 m)

Abraj Al Bait Clock Tower
Mecca, Saudi Arabia
1,971 feet (601 m)

Lotte World Tower
Seoul, South Korea
1,819 feet (555 m)

CTF Finance Centre
Guangzhou, China
1,739 feet (530 m)

Taipei 101
Taipei, Taiwan
1,667 feet (508 m)

Shanghai Tower
Shanghai, China
2,073 feet (632 m)

Ping An Finance Centre
Shenzen, China
1,969 feet (600 m)

One World Trade Center
New York City
1,776 feet (541 m)

Tianjin CTF Finance Centre
Tianjin, China
1,739 feet (530 m)

World Financial Center
Shanghai, China
1,614 feet (492 m)

The shape of the Burj Khalifa is based on a desert flower. There are three outer structures grouped around a central tower. The outer sections are built out further at the bottom. As the building rises, the outer sections are set further in, so the Burj Khalifa gets narrower the higher it goes. This reduces the effect of the wind on the structure. Eventually, the outer sections stop and the central tower continues to rise on its own. At the very top is a tall, thin spire.

The Burj Khalifa has a strong upside-down Y-shape, meaning that it's wider at the base than the top.

WHERE'S THE TOP?

People disagree on how to measure tall buildings. Some say that they should be measured at the very highest point. Others argue that spires and antennae should not count in the height of a building. Still others say they should be measured to the highest usable floor—its "occupied height." The area above a skyscraper's occupied height is known as "vanity height."

In 2007 experts decided that the official height should be measured from the ground to the "architectural top." This includes spires but not antennae. If the Burj Khalifa's vanity height was not counted, it would be more than 800 feet (244 m) shorter. It would still be the tallest building in the world—but just barely. And it would lose its "megatall" status.

No one had ever designed a building anywhere near this tall before. The architects and engineers had to rethink the way skyscrapers were built. The Burj Khalifa has many features that had never been seen before. Some of the most important are the special safety features. Usually in emergencies, such as a fire or earthquake, the elevators in a building stop working. But the Burj Khalifa's elevators have a "lifeboat" mode. This means they can work on emergency power from generators. The elevators are also water resistant, so they will still work if the sprinklers go off in a fire.

The Burj Khalifa was the first of a new generation of megatall buildings, but already there are plans for even taller structures. The skyscrapers of the future might be taller than we can even imagine—just as the height of the Burj Khalifa would have seemed impossible to the men who designed and built the very first skyscrapers.

The Burj Khalifa's observation deck is 1,823 feet (556 m) high.

GLOSSARY

diagonal (dye-AG-uh-nuhl)—joining opposite corners of a square or rectangle

engineer (en-juh-NEER)—someone trained to design and build machines, vehicles, bridges, roads, or other structures

flying buttress (FLY-ing BUHT-ris)—an arched structure that extends beyond a wall or building and supports it

foundation (foun-DAY-shuhn)—a base on which something rests or is built

gargoyle (GAHR-goil)—an animal head or figure carved out of stone

girder (GUR-dur)—a large, heavy beam made of steel or concrete and used in construction

Gothic (GAH-thik)—a style of art or architecture used in western Europe between the 1100s and 1500s that featured tall towers, arches, and stained-glass windows

hydraulic (hye-DRAW-lik)—powered by fluid forced through pipes or chambers

limestone (LYM-stohn)—a hard rock formed from the remains of ancient sea creatures

piling (PYL-ing)—a heavy wood or steel pole or beam that is driven into the ground to support a building, bridge, or pier

reinforce (ree-in-FORSS)—to strengthen the structure or shape of something

retaining wall (ree-TAYN-ing WAWL)—a wall that is built to keep the land behind it from sliding

shaft (SHAFT)—a long, narrow passage that goes straight down

superstructure (SOO-per-struhk-chur)—the part of a building that is above the foundation or lowest part

ventilation system (ven-tuh-LAY-shuhn SIS-tuhm)—a system that allows the flow of fresh air

READ MORE

Duke, Shirley. *Skyscrapers and Towers*. Engineering Wonders. Vero Beach, Fla.: Rourke Educational Media, 2015.

Marsico, Katie. *Skyscrapers*. A True Book. Scholastic, 2016.

Schmermund, Elizabeth. *Explore Skyscrapers!: With 25 Great Projects*. Explore Your World. White River Junction, Vt.: Nomad Press, 2018.

Spray, Sally. *Skyscrapers*. Awesome Engineering. North Mankato, Minn.: Capstone Press, 2018.

INTERNET SITES

Use FactHound to find Internet site related to this book.

Visit www.facthound.com

Just type in 9781543529067 and go.

CRITICAL THINKING QUESTIONS

1. Explain what foundations are, how they are usually built, and why they are so important in building design.

2. Imagine you are a newspaper reporter in New York in 1902. Write an article about the Flatiron Building that is under construction in the city. Include information about why it is being built and where. Comment on its unusual shape and materials. Include quotations from local people.

3. List several factors that architects and engineers have to consider when designing a skyscraper. Consider structure, internal and external forces, and environmental issues. Which do you think are the most important? Does this change depending on where the skyscraper is located or what it will be used for? Give examples from the text to support your ideas.

Super-cool stuff! Check out projects, games and lots more at
www.capstonekids.com

INDEX